NAVMC 2688

COMMANDER'S GUIDE
TO
INSTALLATION MANAGEMENT

PCN 100 013376 00

HEADQUARTERS, UNITED STATES MARINE CORPS
2 NAVY ANNEX
WASHINGTON, DC 20380-1775

13 JANUARY 1997

FOREWORD

Installation management is a complex business ranging from daily facilities maintenance and emergency services to long range planning for construction and encroachment control. In our Headquarters role of providing the Commandant's centralized direction and oversight for installation management, it is our responsibility to provide you resources and tools to help you ensure our bases and stations are equipped to be the "launch platforms" for our operating forces.

You are in the business of providing the quality facilities and excellent services that directly impact the readiness, relevance and capabilities of Marines and Sailors committed in harm's way. These facilities and services cannot be separated from our combat forces. They are the elements of the Marine Corps installations from which we project our forces.

Your challenges are diverse, complex and expanding. The increasing cost of doing business competes with your role as resource manager, environmental steward and neighbor to the surrounding communities. But above all, you retain the commitment to provide a quality environment in which our Marine families live, work, and train.

I am providing this reference to help you meet your "city manager" challenges. I am confident it will help address many of your daily and long range facilities and services issues.

E. B. HAILSTON
Brigadier General, U. S. Marine Corps
Assistant Deputy Chief of Staff for
Installations and Logistics (Facilities)

COMMANDER'S GUIDE TO FACILITIES MANAGEMENT FUNCTIONS

CONTENTS

PAGE

INTRODUCTION 1

COMMAND AND FUNCTIONS 3

CONSTRUCTION PLANNING AND PROGRAMMING 7

REAL ESTATE AND INVENTORY 11

REAL PROPERTY MAINTENANCE ACTIVITIES
AND SPECIAL PROGRAMS 15

UNACCOMPANIED PERSONNEL HOUSING 31

FAMILY HOUSING 35

NATURAL RESOURCES 41

ENVIRONMENTAL QUALITY 43

FOOD SERVICE AND SUBSISTENCE 47

GARRISON PROPERTY 51

GARRISON MOBILE EQUIPMENT 53

TRAFFIC MANAGEMENT 55

INSTALLATION EXCELLENCE PROGRAMS 59

POINTS OF CONTACT 61

INSTALLATION MANAGEMENT ABBREVIATIONS 63

INTRODUCTION

The intent of this guide is to provide you with a quick reference on matters relating to installation management. It should assist you in:

- determining your local funding authority or limitations;

- addressing facilities and services issues;

- identifying appropriate organizational channels; and

- evaluating installation management effectiveness.

A brief summary is provided by functional area highlighting the key points. Included is a list of potential questions you might use when visiting the various facilities and services organizations on your installation to "see how things are going."

COMMAND AND FUNCTIONS

As commanding general (CG) /commanding officer (CO), you are responsible for the adequacy and condition of all facilities and related supporting services. A staff organization has been proposed to effectively manage and advise on installation matters. The organization and titles vary among activities because of local preferences. The most common title of the staff officer directly responsible for management of facilities programs is the Director of Facilities or the Assistant Chief of Staff, Facilities Management. In some instances the functions are under an Assistant Chief of Staff, G4. Transportation, food service, and garrison property are most often under the Assistant Chief of Staff, Logistics.

MCO P11000.16 refers (see Chart i). The responsibilities of the Director of Facilities are normally as follows:

    Facilities Planning and Programming
    Real Estate and Inventory
    Real Property Maintenance Activities (Some subfunctions
       (e.g., fire protection) may be under another staff agency)
    Bachelor Housing
    Family Housing
    Natural Resources
    Energy Conservation
    Environmental Quality

NOTIONAL ORGANIZATIONAL DIAGRAM

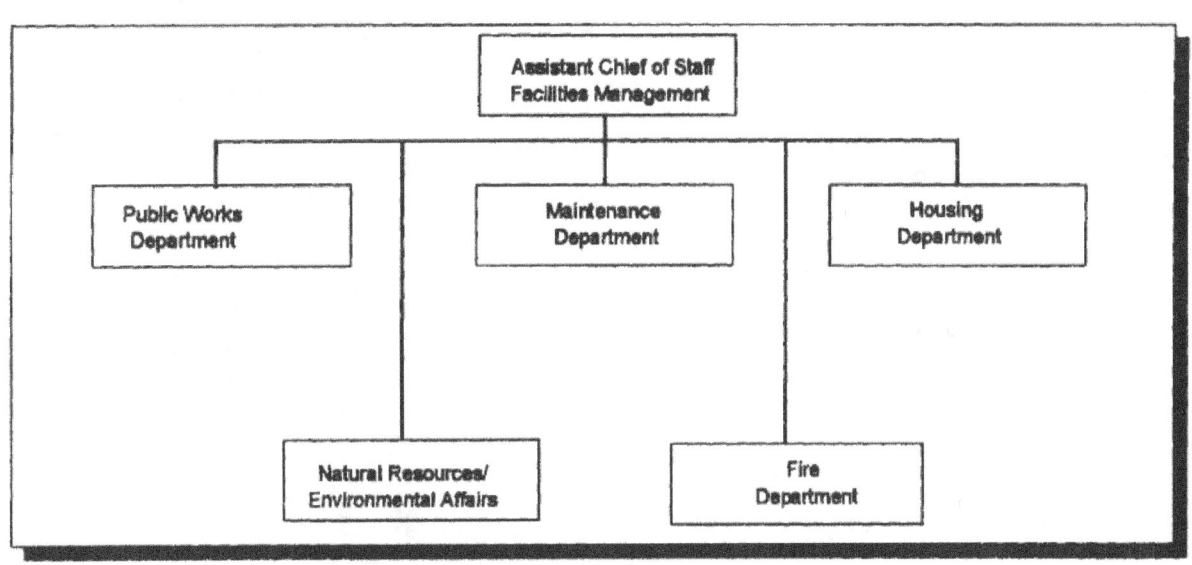

Chart 1

The supporting staff to accomplish these functions varies with size and local desires of the activity commander but the organization includes a manager and personnel for:

Facilities planning, programming, inventory, and engineering
Facilities maintenance, utility operation, fire prevention and control, and supporting services.
Natural resources and environmental management.
Housing management

Additional technical assistance is available from the Naval Facilities Engineering Command (NAVFAC) engineering field divisions (EFD), usually referred to as EFD's. The EFD's that support the Marine Corps major activities are as follows:

EFD	Location	Servicing
Northern Division	Philadelphia, Pennsylvania	Marine Corps Support Activity, Kansas City, Missouri; First Marine Corps District, Garden City, New York
Atlantic Division	Norfolk, Virginia	Marine Corps Air Station, Cherry Point, North Carolina; Marine Corps Base, Camp Lejeune, North Carolina
Chesapeake Division (Engineering Field Activity)	Washington, DC	Marine Corps Combat Development Command, Quantico, Virginia (see note 1); Headquarters Battalion, Henderson Hall, Arlington, Virginia; and Marine Barracks, 8th & I, Washington, DC

EFD	Location	Servicing
Southern Division	Charleston, South Carolina	Marine Corps Recruit Depot, Eastern Recruiting Region, Parris Island, South Carolina; Marine Corps Air Station, Beaufort, South Carolina; Marine Corps Logistics Base, Albany, Georgia; and MarForRes, 4th Mar Division/Aircraft Wing, New Orleans, Louisiana
Southwest Division	San Diego, California	Marine Corps Base Camp Pendleton, California; Mountain Warfare Training Center, Bridgeport, California; Marine Corps Recruit Depot/Western Recruiting Region, San Diego, California; Marine Corps Air Station, Camp Pendleton, California; Marine Corps Air Station, El Toro, California; Marine Corps Logistics Base, Barstow, California; Marine Corps Air Ground Combat Center, Twentynine Palms, California; Marine Corps Air Station, Yuma, Arizona; Marine Corps Air Station, Tustin, California; Naval Air Station, Marine Corps Air Station, Miramar, California

EFD	Location	Servicing
Pacific Division	Honolulu, Hawaii	All Marine Corps bases, Pacific (except Fire Marshal Services which are provided by CINCPACFLT)

The preceding EFD's will respond to any type of facilities engineering problem and to some management problems. In the event the expertise or manpower is not available within the EFD they will undertake the work by contract (see note 2).

NOTES:

1. Fire Marshal Service is provided by Atlantic Division and Pest Control Service by Northern Division.

2. Substantial lead-time should be provided. Anticipate 90 to 120 days at a minimum to obtain a contract.

CONSTRUCTION PLANNING AND PROGRAMMING

From conception to beneficial occupancy of a new facility usually requires 4 to 5 years. This cannot normally be accomplished in one tour of duty.

New facilities are conceived and obtained per the provisions of MCO P11000.12. The basis for facilities development is a master plan developed for the activity by the local EFD or by contract. The master plan is a general use strategy showing the land and facility uses by area. It includes a capital improvements plan showing planned construction and an ultimate land use plan. Related factors to be considered in planning are land use compatibility, National Environmental Policy Act (NEPA), the Air Installation Compatible Use Zone (AICUZ), encroachment, and Coastal Zone Planning. The master plan is updated on a 6-year cycle and is approved by the Commandant of the Marine Corps (CMC) (LF).

PLANNING

Each planning cycle starts with the publication of the Facilities Support Requirements (FSR) Planning Document. The dynamic document provides base commanders and FMF command element commanders with detailed lists of projected base loading, tasks, new equipment, and units for each activity. Your facility planning staff translates the base loading data of the FSR into basic facility requirements (BFR). The requirements are listed by category code on Form NAVMC 10915 (BFR Item Determination Sheet). A complete set of Form NAVMC 10915 constitutes total facility requirements in overall items (e.g., so many square feet of warehouse, administration, classroom, etc., required to provide for the unit's personnel and equipment shown in the FSR). Knowing what your needs are, the next step is to apply available assets; i.e., the information contained within the Navy Facility Assets Data Base (NFADB) (Form NAVMC 10651) against these needs. The NFADB is available from the Facilities Systems Office (FACSO), Port Hueneme, California. Changes to the NFADB are derived from the changes to property records which you send to FACSO, or input directly if your activity has on-line access to FACSO. With the knowledge of needs and the assets to apply against these needs, the activity commander formulates a plan to construct new facilities, convert excess facilities to eliminate deficiencies, or to dispose of excess facilities. This plan is tabulated by category code on Facilities Planning Documents (FPD). FPD's are the basis for the development of projects and are generated automatically at FACSO. Planning data is direct input by your activity through on-line access. Projects funded by Military Construction, Navy (MCON), nonappropriated fund (NAF), Operations and Maintenance, Marine Corps (O&MMC), Family

Housing, Navy and Marine Corps (FHN&MC), etc., are listed on the Summary for Correction of Facility Deficiencies (form NAVMC 10956). For urgent and unforeseeable facility requirements; relocatable facilities may be approved by the CMC for up to 3 years pending permanent construction completion.

PROGRAMMING

Construction programming instructions are provided biennially by the Military Construction Planning and Programming Guidance Letter which is an adjunct to MCO P11000.12. This letter requests that you recommend and prioritize a 6-year construction program at your activity and identify any other construction requirements at your activity. The current 6-year program is included as part of this guidance letter and should be used as a framework for developing a new 6-year program. In addition to your prioritized program, backup programming documents (such as DD1391's and environmental documentation) are also requested. The EFD (discussed below) can assist in the preparation of backup programming documentation on a cost reimbursable basis.

After receipt of your project documentation and recommendations your activity is invited to present the first 2 years of the revised 6-year program to the Military Construction Planning and Evaluation Group (MilCon PEG). The MilCon PEG consists of representatives of the HQMC Staff from I&L, ASL, P&R, M&RA and CG, MCCDC (T&E). Based on your priority recommendations, and project documentation, the MilCon PEG prioritizes, then merges all Marine Corps construction requirements and recommends a total program that is reviewed and approved through the HQMC Program Objective Memorandum (POM) budgeting process.

Execution of the MilCon program is accomplished by the Department of the Navy (DON) construction agent NAVFAC (Naval Facilities Engineering Command), who delegates this authority to the EFD. The management of the construction contract is, in turn, delegated to a local resident officer in charge of construction (ROICC). The ROICC, who reports to the EFD commander, is on site to properly administer all construction contracts, including those that you generate at your activity.

Urgent construction requirements that cost between $300,000 and $1.5M ($3M for projects that correct life, health, or safety threats) and cannot wait for the regular MilCon program may be developed and processed as unspecified minor construction (UMC) projects. A UMC project, per Title 10 of the U.S. Code, must be prompted by one of the following situations:

- New primary mission
- Unexpected growth in existing primary missions.
- Hazard to life and property
- Regulatory or statutory requirements.

8

- <u>Unexpected</u> new items of major equipment
- <u>Unexpected</u> loss of, or severe reduction in, supporting utility sources or Systems that will jeopardize the ability to continue performance of (the activity's) primary mission.

CONSTRUCTION PLANNING AND PROGRAMMING QUESTIONS

1. Do we have a CMC approved Master Plan?

2. Has the Master Plan been updated in the last 6 years? If not, is an update required?

3. Do we forward to HQMC BFR's (basic facility requirement) after receipt of the FSR every January and whenever a revision to the BFR's is needed?

4. Is a new FPD requested from FACSO whenever the presently held one has been changed by construction, demolition, or changes in building use?

5. Are we using local EFD assets for engineering help in the development of projects and facility planning? Are they responsive?

6. Do we ensure that only minor changes, those that do not impact on land use or general base development, are being made to the Master Plan locally?

7. What is the status of MilCon projects not under construction? Are facilities studies with economic and environmental analyses complete and up to date?

8. What MilCon projects do we currently have under construction?

9. Have we reviewed and updated the FSR to reflect the most current personnel strength and equipment changes?

10. Have these changes been forwarded to the CMC (LFL)?

11. Is the FSR used by the planning staff as a working document in their facilities planning functions?

12. Are we using relocatable facilities? If so, what is the status of their replacement with permanent construction?

13. Have potential environmental impacts been considered and documented?

REAL ESTATE AND INVENTORY

REAL ESTATE

With very few exceptions, real estate actions involving a party outside the Marine Corps are executed by NAVFAC through the EFD having responsibility for a particular geographical area. As there are many different kinds of acquisition, disposal, and outgrant actions stemming from a wide variety of authorities and requiring diverse approval levels, you should consult with CMC (LFL) whenever a real estate action is anticipated. Real estate activities are covered in MCO P11000.14 and NAVFAC P-73, Real Estate Procedural Manual.

Except for those real estate actions mandated by the preceding authorities, all real estate actions require your approval. The technical services that the EFD furnishes to accomplish real estate actions can only be effective if based on complete knowledge of the needs, objectives, and conditions of the activity. Hence, all accomplishments in this area depend upon cooperation of you, the CMC, and the EFD.

Some real estate issues may require legal review, which can be obtained from the respective Marine Corps regional counsel offices: Eastern Area Counsel Office (EACO), Camp Lejeune and Western Area Counsel Office (WACO), Camp Pendleton.

ENCROACHMENT

As an activity commander, you must be constantly aware that Marine Corps interests do not end at the activity fence line. Proposed land use actions initiated by the civilian community, county, State, and other Federal agencies can greatly affect the base; e.g., residential/commercial/industrial development, transportation, construction, recreational development, aircraft transportation systems, environmental, and natural resources conservation laws can encroach upon an activity's ability to carry out its mission. Early detection of potential encroachment and careful assessment of likely impacts are essential.

Accordingly, the Commandant has implemented two initiatives to identify and contain incompatible land use around our bases. First, the East and West Coast General Officer Regional Review Boards meets to review and correlate individual mission requirements to ensure no conflicts exist, and to identify and analyze potential encroachment issues that arise in the local communities.

Second, you must effectively manage an Encroachment Control Program as described in MCO 11011.22. The success of this program requires a productive working relationship with local officials; i.e., a two-way interchange of information on land use issues.

Another, although seemingly harmless policy, is our practice to outgrant land which is not currently being used by the Marine Corps but is not excess to our needs. If the outgrantee is an influential party, such as a civil or religious organization and their use has been long-standing, it can be very difficult or politically impossible to revoke their use of base property. Accordingly, you must obtain HQMC approval prior to making a commitment to provide real property interests to individuals or entities outside the Department of Defense (DoD) (excluding short-term licenses and permits of one-year or less duration).

GSA REAL PROPERTY UTILIZATION SURVEY

By Executive Order, the General Services Administration (GSA), on a continuing basis, conducts surveys of real property holdings of executive agencies to identify properties which are not used, are under-used, or are not being put to their optimum use. When GSA conducts such a survey, it often concludes, merely on the basis of a preliminary review or scouting report, that there is insufficient utilization of land or facilities. To correct erroneous evaluations, GSA teams should be thoroughly briefed on the command mission, mission and training requirements, and property management and utilization. This education can markedly increase the probability of retaining needed land. Technical assistance in preparing for these surveys is available from the CMC (LFL). In any event, HQMC should be notified immediately upon notice from GSA of such a survey. The CMC (LFL) will assist the activity in preparing for a GSA survey and also send a representative to participate in the on-site survey.

If the CMC (LFL) cannot overturn GSA's recommendation for disposal action, you should consider that the Marine Corps could lose all authority over such land. You should further consider that the Marine Corps will continue to fund and provide for maintenance and security of the property for at least 12 to 15 months after the property reported excess to GSA has been accepted by that agency. After that time, the funding requirement may be accepted by GSA.

INVENTORY

Two very important functions concerning real estate are maintenance of current and accurate summary maps of the landholdings of the activity and a current and accurate real property inventory.

The inventory is maintained by NAVFAC through FACSO at Port Hueneme, California. Data for the inventory is maintained by the activity or forwarded directly to the FACSO as changes occur. At intervals, mechanized printouts are provided to all activities. The responsibility for developing the inventory at the activity level is normally assigned to the engineering staff and the comptroller.

Annually, shortly after the close of a fiscal year, the activity is provided copies of NAVFAC P-164 which lists all class I (land) and II (facilities) property at the activity as of the prior 30 September. The inventory will provide much useful data such as the category code, facility type, year acquired or constructed, cost to Government, current plant value, area dimensions, and the property record number.

REAL ESTATE AND INVENTORY QUESTIONS

1. Is the Land Utilization Plan current?

2. Can the Land Utilization Plan be defended if an Executive Order 12512 Survey is conducted at this base?

3. Does the base have an effective Encroachment Control Program?

4. Could the mission of our activity be fulfilled at other Marine Corps/Government-owned land?

5. Will the outgranting of land or buildings affect future plans?

6. Are all present uses of land and/or buildings by individuals, corporations, etc., and other Federal agencies covered by a real estate agreement?

7. What are these agreements and licenses?

8. Does a Request for Acquisition of Land address environmental impacts?

9. Has a commitment been made for use or disposal of Marine Corps property which may not be consistent with existing laws?

10. Have HQMC and the EFD been informed concerning all transactions dealing with real estate?

11. Will the acquisition or disposal under consideration affect any historical site?

12. What is the estimated degree of accuracy of the Real Property Inventory? How can it be improved?

13. Do we get good response from the EFD for updating NAVFAC P-164?

14. Does our activity have a standing procedure for updating the inventory?

15. Do we have as-built plans for all facilities and utility systems?

REAL PROPERTY MAINTENANCE ACTIVITIES (RPMA)
AND SPECIAL PROGRAMS

The RPMA's are the functions that must be performed to maintain and operate our bases. They include the following three categories:

Maintenance, repair, and minor construction of real property.

Purchase, production, distribution, and operation of utilities.

Other engineering services (installation management services, solid waste collection, disposal and recycling, custodial services, fire prevention and suppression, and technical engineering)

MAINTENANCE AND REPAIR

The Maintenance and Repair (MRP) program begins with identification of what needs to be fixed and the recurring maintenance that needs to be done on a routine basis to keep the facilities operating. Fully funding recurring maintenance is the key to the long term operational readiness of your facilities.

Recurring maintenance includes inspecting and patching roofs, lubricating machinery, sealing pavements, changing filters, exterior painting, etc. It is this work that allows us to ensure our facilities reach their full economic life at the lowest possible cost. Unfortunately, recurring maintenance is often deferred because the impact is not immediate. You probably have urgent repairs that need to be done, some of which are affecting mission operations. If you check, you will find many of these repairs could have been avoided by adequate recurring maintenance.

For example, roofs with a small amount of yearly inspection and repair, will last 15 to 20 years. But, if this yearly maintenance is ignored, the same roofs will only last 8 to 10 years. This almost doubles the cost of keeping the roofs on your buildings.

Inspections are done by your maintenance office. They either perform the inspections in-house or contract them out. This inspection provides one of the key inputs to your annual work plan and long range maintenance plan. The annual work plan includes what work should be performed in the current year if MRP was fully funded. The long range maintenance plan covers unconstrained MRP requirements for the next 5 years.

The annual work plan readily converts into a fiscally constrained annual work program when the funding is known and MRP requirements are prioritized.

The work that remains to be done from the annual work plan because of lack of funding becomes the Backlog of Maintenance and Repair (BMAR). This backlog is the result of several factors:

    The effectiveness of your inspection program.

    The resources you had available.

    The commitment to fully funding routine maintenance.

It is extremely important that all of your valid maintenance and repair requirements are identified and reported in your Annual Work Plan, Long Range Maintenance Plan, and BMAR reports.

The BMAR reports, in particular, must provide an accurate portrayal of all the maintenance and repair work you should have already accomplished but could not because of a lack of resources.

The reason the BMAR reports are so important is that HQMC, Office of the Secretary of Defense (OSD), Secretary of the Navy (SecNav) and Congress all use BMAR as a yardstick to measure the condition of our installations and as the basis for making resource procurement and allocation decisions.

It might be helpful to think of BMAR as an iceberg, with reported deficiencies above the water line, and undetected, unreported needs below the surface. Your goal should be to ensure that all reported needs are valid, and that you have an absolute minimum number of undetected/unreported requirements. Other facilities maintenance and repair matters you should be aware of are:

    Your activity BMAR Report is due to Headquarters by 10 October of each year. The report is updated annually.

    Of the MRP funds provided in the financial ceilings, a goal of a maximum of 6 percent is established for locally approved minor construction projects.

    Additional details on the maintenance and repair program are contained in MCO P11000.7 and MCO P11000.5.

Contract Advertisement Forecast: Two times a year, 15 March and 15 September, your command sends a prioritized list of projects to the CMC (LFF). This list lets HQMC know which of your approved projects will be ready to execute in the next 6 to 9 months.

These lists are our primary tool for selecting projects for execution. Command priority plays a heavy role in HOMC's selection.

REAL PROPERTY MAINTENANCE/FAMILY HOUSING SYSTEM (RPM/FHS)

RPM/FHS is a management information system designed to provide the RPM and family housing activities automation required for effective management of their organizations. RPM/FHS is a class I B standard system. The system provides the following capabilities:

RPM

Receive, track, and close out service work;

Receive, estimate, track, and schedule work requests;

Maintain detailed facilities histories;

Automate the BMAR and Work Plan/Programs;

Monitor contracts and projects;

Automate supply and inventory accounting.

Family Housing

Automate housing waiting lists;

Automate scheduling of housing units;

Automate housing inspections;

Track customer status and charges;

Automate off-base housing referral services.

General

Provide local report generation capabilities.

SUPPLY SUPPORT FOR FACILITIES MAINTENANCE

Effective supply and material support are crucial to efficient in-house facilities maintenance (FM) operations. To achieve this efficiency of operations, FM needs to function in an environment similar to the one in which the private business sector operates.

Your facilities maintenance officer (FMO) should consider the following source for obtaining required supplies and materials in the most effective combination of price, quality, and responsiveness:

Standard supply Systems operated by the activity Direct Support Stock Control Center (DSSC), to include Navy versions handled by the Naval Supply System Command (NAVSUP) and the GSA Customer Supply Center.

Property Disposal Offices operated by the Defense Reutilization and Marketing Office (DRMO).

Open purchase through means of Indefinite Delivery/Quantity Type Contracts (ID/QTC), Blanket Purchase Agreements (BPA), and Individual Requisitions.

The FMO needs to establish a close working relationship with your purchasing and contracting officer (P&CO) to obtain ID/QTC's and BPA's; and if designated, an ordering officer will place calls against ID/QTC's and BPA's. Management responsibilities for FM material and supply support are outlined in MCO Pl1000.7, chapter 7.

REAL PROPERTY MAINTENANCE ACTIVITIES QUESTIONS

1. What is the status of the long range maintenance plan?

2. What control inspection work is done by contract; should it be more or less?

3. What is the facilities maintenance department personnel ceiling?

4. Do you have any personnel ceiling problems?

5. Are there any key positions unfilled?

6. Have all facilities been inspected according to your Control Inspection Program? If not, why?

7. What is the annual budget for FM? What is the activity maintenance of real property target?

8. What reimbursable customers do you have? What is the order or magnitude for maintenance and repair for reimbursable customers?

9. Are there delays in getting work requests accomplished?

10. What is the backlog of work for shops?

11. How is the priority of work established?

12. What is the BMAR? Is it increasing?

13. Have all outstanding inspection deficiencies been included in the BMAR Report and identified on the Projects Plan?

14. Am I participating in the BMAR Report and Projects Plan and minor construction project selection by setting command priorities?

15. Is obtaining supplies or materials a problem?

16. Has the FMO been delegated authority on source of supply to be used to best fulfill FM needs?

17. Has the P&CO instituted ID/QTC and BPA contracts to support FM? Have FM materials support people been designated as ordering officers to place calls against ID/QTC's and BPA's?

18. What kind of preventive and cyclic maintenance programs do we have?

19. How is emergency service (ES) work handled? What is the current backlog?

20. Are engineered performance standards (EPS) used to measure work performance? How closely are standards met?

21. Is the percent of the maintenance budget spent on alterations and minor construction within the ceiling authorized by HQMC?

22. If activity has tenants, are host-tenant agreements and interservice support agreements (ISA) available and periodically reviewed for updating?

23. Are customers satisfied with the service? Are they kept advised on status of their requests?

24. What training programs do we have for our FM people?

25. Do we have an apprentice training program?

26. Do we have a union contract?

27. Have there been any grievances recently? Pending problems?

28. What are the overhead costs in the FM Department? Can they be reduced?

29 Are shop spaces, tools, and equipment adequate? Are shop tools, equipment, and left over materials properly accounted for?

30. Are additional maintenance and operating funds and personnel requirements being put in our budget for newly constructed facilities?

31. Do we have a Facility Demolition Program?

32. Does the activity have a Self-Help Program using local military and dependent personnel to accomplish real property maintenance, repair, equipment installation, and new minor construction work?

33. Are qualified representatives from facilities maintenance provided to lend technical and professional assistance to personnel engaged in self-help work?

34. Has a local directive been published containing Self-Help Program information such as: instruction encouraging tenant commanders1 participation; types of work eligible; and the system for requesting, approving, and monitoring projects?

35. Does the activity have established procedures to identify Self-Help Program costs?

36. Does the activity participate in the Silver Hammer Self-Help Award Program?

CENTRALLY MANAGED FACILITIES PROJECTS PROGRAMS

The Centrally Managed Facilities Projects Program is administered by HQMC. The major repair (M-2) and minor construction (R-2) projects funded and accomplished under this program have costs which exceed the activity commander's approval authority. Most of the projects in the program are accomplished by contract.

The program is developed from the major repair deficiencies identified on the fiscally unconstrained BMAR Reports and Projects Plan submitted annually by your activity to the CMC (LFF) by 10 October and the Annual Listing of Minor Construction Projects also submitted annually by 10 October. The deficiencies are surveyed on site by HQMC representatives and are scored against a series of criteria including local command priorities. The scores are used to prioritize each project in relation to similar projects across the Marine Corps.

Based on a projection of available resources, the CMC (LFF) selects the highest priority projects. You are then notified of those projects so you may begin this engineering and design work to produce the plans and specifications to accomplish the work by contract. For those projects which have plans and specification completed, HQMC will, if resources are available, authorize advertising and provide funds for the work to be accomplished. The large factor in deciding which projects will be funded is the priority you place on the contract advertisement forecast submitted to HQMC in September and March.

For large, complex, high interest projects, you may be required to submit plans and specifications for HQMC review before authority to advertise is granted. (for example: whole building rehabilitation of administration facilities)

Following contract award, projects may require changes to the work due to unforeseen site conditions, design errors, design omissions, or other reasons. You are authorized to approve and fund changes within an established contingency provided by HQMC for each project. The contingency varies for each project but will not exceed 15 percent of the contract price. Current or prior year appropriations are used to fund changes, as required.

Near the end of each fiscal year, HQMC authorizes a group of projects to be advertised that can be awarded either in the current or next fiscal year. We call this our "straddle" program. By "straddling" two fiscal years, the Marine Corps ensures obligation of all available current year O&MMC resources and positions itself for early obligation of a portion of its following year O&MMC resources toward high priority MRP requirements.

Specific policy, procedure, and guidance on the M2/R2 projects program are contained in MCO P11000.5.

FACILITIES PROJECTS QUESTIONS

1. What projects are currently included in the facilities projects program?

2. Can any prior year unfunded projects be deleted?

3. What projects are under design for the next 2 years?

4. How many projects having plans and specifications are available for year-end funding?

5. Are project submittals in sufficient detail with drawings, photographs, etc., to express scope and justifications?

6. What is the usual timeframe from HQMC survey of the project to time of accomplishment?

7. Do we have a good rapport with the EFD?

8. Do we solicit EFD help on technical matters? Statutory and regulatory matters?

9. Who is the HQMC contact for approval/funding of projects?

10. When was the last time you made personal contact with the HQMC contact?

11. Where are the bottlenecks in executing the program?

12. Do we have an internal system for developing, preparing, and submitting projects?

13. Can we improve our projects program?

14. What is the "dollar limit" of my authority for minor construction?

15. How long after receiving HQMC authority to advertise, is the project actually advertised and awarded?

FACILITIES MAINTENANCE AND REPAIR

The following is a chart showing delegations of authority for maintenance, repair, and construction work financed from O&MMC resources at major Marine Corps shore activities:

APPROVAL AUTHORITY

Type work	Amount to Activity Cdr ($)	Amount HQMC ($)
Repair1/	-0- to 300,000 (M-1)	300,001 to 3,000,000 (M-2)
Construction2/ 3/	-0- to 100,000 (R-1)	100,001 to 300,000 4/ (R-2)

1/ If the cost exceeds $300,000 and 50 percent replacement value, the SecNav's approval is required

2/ Above $300,000 refer to construction planning and programming section of this Guide, and MCO P11000.12.

3/ Total R-1 expenditures per fiscal year is targeted at 6 percent of the maintenance and repair and minor construction funds provided (6 percent MRP)

4/ Supervision, Inspection, and Overhead (SIOH) cost of 8 percent. Actual contract for construction cannot exceed $276,000.

UTILITIES MANAGEMENT AND ENERGY CONSERVATION

The overall objective of utilities management is to procure, produce, deliver and maintain the utilities needed to meet mission requirements with minimum waste at the lowest possible life-cycle cost and in an environment that provides adequate levels of comfort. The basic directive is MCO P11000.9, Real Property Facilities Manual, Volume VI, Energy and Utilities Management.

Mandates for energy and water conservation have been established by legislation and Executive Order. These include reducing the energy use rate in facilities by 20 percent by FY 2000, and by 30 percent by FY 2005, compared to FY 1985, identifying (through comprehensive audits) and implementing all life-cycle cost effective (payback in 10 years or less) energy and water conservation projects by 2005, and using life-cycle cost analysis procedures to justify all equipment and project selections. You should have an active, aggressive energy and water conservation program that focuses on increasing personnel awareness and on identifying and implementing projects. Annual award programs recognize outstanding conservation achievements. The SECNAV Energy Conservation Award includes a monetary award. The Federal Energy Efficiency and Water Conservation Awards are commendation awards.

Planning is an essential element of successful utilities management. The Utilities Master Plan is a part of the installation Master Plan and generally addresses utility needs in terms of meeting mission goals. The Long-Range Utilities and Energy Plan is a 5-year plan, updated annually, that covers all facets of utilities supply and delivery, conservation, budgeting, procurement, production, operation, maintenance, repair, overhaul, training, construction, and studies and assessments.

The utilities engineer is the focal point for utilities management. Ideally, you should also have a full time energy conservation manager. The Energy Policy Act of 1992 (P.L. 102-486) requires energy managers be proficient in six specific areas. The Utilities Conservation and Appraisal Board (UCAB) acts in an advisory capacity to the installation commander on utilities. It is also responsible for planning and pursuing a progressive conservation program. The UCAB is made up of key representatives of the installation management departments, major tenants, and other offices as appropriate. The utilities engineer should be a member of the UCAB. Engineering Field

Division (EFD) utilities personnel should attend UCAB meetings. Utility procurement contracts are generally negotiated and awarded by your servicing EFD. The UCAB should review utility contracts on a regular basis to ensure the most cost-effective rate schedule is being used.

Establishing and executing a comprehensive maintenance program is essential to ensure safe, reliable, and efficient utilities operations. The inspection program should include the following elements: control inspections, preventive maintenance inspections, cyclic maintenance inspections, operator inspections, and special surveys, audits and assessments. Requirements identified in these inspections are programmed in the annual and long-range utilities plans. Most of the inspection work is conducted in-house. Other sources such as the EFD, the Naval Facilities Engineering Services Center (NFESC), the local public utility, and contractors may be used to meet special requirements.

Several funding programs are available for studies, construction, maintenance, and repair work related to energy and utilities systems:

1. **Energy and Utilities Improvement Program (EUIP).** This program funds studies, surveys, and assessments to identify cost-effective energy and water conservation projects, training related to energy conservation management and utilities operations, and purchase of energy audit equipment and utilities management software. It also funds contract development support for special contracts such as Shared Energy Savings. Fund source: Marine Corps O&M (P-1).

2. **Facilities Projects Program.** This program funds major repair and minor construction projects. Energy and utility projects are a subset of the total centrally managed program. Fund source: Marine Corps O&M (M-2/R-2).

3. **Military Construction Program.** This program funds new construction over $300,000. Fund source: MILCON, Navy.

4. **Energy Conservation Investment Program (ECIP).** This DoD program funds MILCON scope construction in existing buildings that saves energy and/or money. It is programmed separately from other MILCON programs through the CMC (LFF). Fund source: MILCON, Defense Agencies.

5. **Federal Energy Management Program (FEMP).** A DoD program that funds energy conservation retrofit projects that qualify as repair and minor construction projects. Programmed through the CMC (LFF). Fund source: O&M, Defense Agencies.

financing arrangement for obtaining energy efficiency improvements in facilities. Contracts are long-term, up to 25 years, with an energy services company who pays all up-front

6. **Energy Savings Performance Contracts.** This is an alternative costs. In exchange, the contractor receives a share of the cost savings resulting from the improvements. Fund source: Initial capital -- contractor provided. Contractor compensated from share of the savings from O&M utilities funds over negotiated contract term.

Utilities and Energy Reports are required to monitor achievement toward conservation goals, for management assessment of operating performance and for budgeting purposes. Defense Utility and Energy Reports (DUERS) (formerly referred to as DEIS II) are forwarded monthly by each installation to NFESC to report energy cost, consumption, and facility data. NFESC publishes a quarterly Energy Audit Report (EAR) using the DUERS data. The EAR details progress toward the mandated energy use rate reduction. Progress is reported annually to Congress. The annual Utilities Cost Analysis Report (UCAR) (NAVCOMPT Form 2127) shows all costs of utilities and fuels used; quantities of production, purchase, distribution and sales; and the cost/quantity rates of utilities. It is used to establish the Activity Rate that reimbursable customers pay for utilities, as the primary utility budget analysis tool and for calculating figures of merit (performance indicators).

A Utilities Metering Program should be considered for accurately measuring utilities consumption. Validation of the estimates of energy savings made during project development is required for conservation projects funded by DoD. Meters at reimbursable customer boundaries aide in establishing billing amounts.

Security of utility systems and supply is essential for maintaining mission readiness and should be addressed in your Energy/Utilities Vulnerability and Contingency Plans. Plans for potential emergencies and impacts, including shortages or cutbacks required by suppliers in high use periods (load shedding), should be included.

UTILITIES MANAGEMENT AND ENERGY CONSERVATION QUESTIONS

1. Is the facilities organization staffed with a utilities engineer to manage the installation utilities programs?

2. Is energy conservation assigned to one individual as a full time duty and does the individual have the training required by the Energy Policy Act of 1992? Are nominations submitted for recognition in award programs?

3. Will the existing utility Systems meet the projected demand and environmental requirements for the next 5 years? Have corrective actions been initiated to address deficiencies?

4. Has the UCAB been established by installation order and is it functioning?

5. Have utility procurement contracts been reviewed within the last 3 years? Are more favorable rate options available?

6. What is the impact of electric demand charges on the electric utility bill? Is a load management plan in place to control peak demand?

7. Are inspection programs in place to identify maintenance and repair needs and to develop data to support conservation projects?

8. What projects have been completed in the past 2 years and what projects are under development that take advantage of funding sources available? Are utility projects reviewed by the utilities engineer and energy manager as appropriate during early and final design stages?

9. Are monthly DUERS and annual UCAR reports prepared and forwarded? What progress has been made toward the energy use rate reduction goals? Is the UCAR being used to manage the installation utilities budget and support the POM?

10. Is metering in place or planned to validate conservation savings and help manage customer utility billing?

11. Are energy/utility vulnerability and contingency plans in place?

FIRE, RESCUE, AND EMERGENCY SERVICES PROGRAMS

Policy and staffing criteria are contained in MCO P11000.11, Real Property Facilities Manual, volume VIII and other Marine Corps Orders in the 11320 series.

The Marine Corps has two major fire protection program areas:

Fire Protection Engineering Projects Program corrects identified fire safety deficiencies in Marine Corps facilities. MCO P11000.5 describes the annual project submittal, on-site review, and funding process. Program emphasis is placed on life safety projects, smoke detectors and sprinkler systems. NAVFAC EFD's inspect activity buildings and identify, estimate, and report on observed fire discrepancies.

Fire Prevention and Emergency Services Program consists of the fire prevention, education, suppression and rescue services. Command support is key in several areas:

> Fire department review of plans for new and renovated facilities;
> Correcting fire safety conditions identified during inspections;
>
> Maintenance of resources to provide services

Additionally, fire departments provide emergency medical "first responder" services and handle hazardous materials emergencies. Fire departments are headed by a fire chief and organized into fire operations, fire prevention, fire communication, training and administration.

HQMC, DC/S I&L (LFF-1) provides technical assistance, develops policies, and manages the overall program (except crash/fire/ rescue services managed under the Deputy Chief of Staff for Aviation (ASL-45)).

Naval Facilities Engineering Command provides technical assistance, conducts surveys and ensures code compliance in facilities design. NAVFAC also conducts fire marshal inspections of fire departments and investigates all major fires.

Major Requirements (per MCO P11000.11)

Full fire department staffing at all times.

Fire and emergency incident reports submitted to Naval Safety Center.

Fire investigations for all serious fires.

Effective use of fire department resources for complete emergency response capability.

Fire protection projects submitted to correct discrepancies.

Fire marshal inspections done every 2 years.

Timely correction of fire inspection discrepancies.

Fire protection engineering surveys every 5 years.

FIRE PROTECTION/PREVENTION QUESTIONS

1. Are fire inspections discrepancies corrected on time?

2. Is the fire department included in pre-construction/plans reviews for new construction and major renovations?

3. Is an effective public fire education program in place?

RECYCLING PROGRAM

Oversight responsibility for the Marine Corps recycling program is administered by HQMC (LFF-1). The program directives and guidance are contained in MCO P5090.2, Environmental Compliance and Protection Manual and requires that all Marine Corps activities implement source separation for recycling and establish a Qualified Recycling Program (QRP).

Purpose. QRP's are established to:

Comply with Federal, State, and local environmental laws and regulations. If there is a conflict between regulatory requirements, the more stringent requirements prevail.

Avoid excessive costs for disposal of solid waste by other means.

Improve operational efficiency by the reuse of readily available resources.

Obtain proceeds from recyclable material sales.

A QRP consists of a base order/instruction and a specifically designated DRMO (property disposal) account number. Your installation instruction will include the designation of a QRP Manager. Generally, this person is from the department responsible for the management of waste material such as Facilities Engineering/Public Works. Morale, Welfare, and Recreation (MWR) may also serve in this capacity. Your installation, will only begin to receive 100 percent of the proceeds derived from the sale of recycled material upon establishment of a QRP. Proceeds will be used to reimburse all expenses to include employee salaries and improvements to the recycling program such as equipment purchases.

Requirements. Public Law 97-214 stipulates that:

- Up to 50 percent of the proceeds, after expenses, may be used at the installation for pollution abatement, energy conservation, and occupational safety and health activities within the specific limits prescribed for use of O&MMC funds.

- The remaining balance may be transferred to your nonappropriated MWR activities of the installation as defined in existing DON regulations.

- If the balance available to you at the end of any fiscal year is in excess of $2M, the amount of the excess shall go to the Treasury as miscellaneous receipts.

Procedures. When you "sell" recycled materials, those funds are deposited into your recycling account at HQMC (RF). To use those funds, the Recycling Planning Board (which is designated on your base order/instruction and is comprised of various key base representatives) convenes to determine the desired and permissible distribution of a portion of all of the funds accrued. You then submit a request for the funding desired with a breakdown of the planned expenditures to HQMC (LFF-1). Upon review to ensure public law requirements have been met, HQMC (LFF-1) will notify HQMC (RF) to allocate the appropriate funding.

RECYCLING QUESTIONS

1. Is there a designated Recycling Program Manager?

2. Is the program run by Facilities or MWR?

3. Do we have our own landfill or do we have off-base disposal?

4. What kind of industrial and residential materials are we recycling?

5. Are there other types of recycling that we should be instituting?

6. What kind of response are we getting from the base participants and the community?

7. How much money is this program saving us (reduced disposal costs and extended landfill life expectancy)?

8. How much have we reduced (by weight) the amount of materials being disposed?

9. Are we making money? How much?

10. What kind of expenditures have we had thus far?

11. How much money do we currently have in our account?

12. Where do we want to be with this program in the short-term and long-term?

13. Are we submitting the Solid Waste Annual Report (SWAR) to NFESC?

UNACCOMPANIED PERSONNEL HOUSING (UPH)

General Management. It is the policy of DoD and the Marine Corps that UPH accommodations meet the basic physiological and psychological needs, and provide the space, privacy, and furnishings required for comfortable living. It is the CMC's intent that the quality of life for Marines living in BEQ's be improved through better management and more enlightened policies. First-rate living quarters is a priority. The Marine Corps has four specific UEPH goals: (1) Eliminate the current inventory of inadequate Bachelor Quarters; (2) Eliminate the backlog of maintenance and repair for Bachelor Quarters; (3) Obtain maximum utilization of adequate Bachelor Quarters; (4) Improve the quality of Bachelor Quarters furnishings.

Inventory and Utilization Data. The base is required to submit the UPH Inventory and Utilization Data (DD Form 2085) quarterly. This data shows the activity's inventory (rooms are measured in 90 **nsf** increments) and how the rooms are being utilized. It also provides other supplemental data regarding off-base billeting of unaccompanied personnel and geographic bachelors aboard the activity.

Personnel Support Equipment (PSE). A minimum allowance of PSE for UEPH and UOPH has been established and is to be provided for all unaccompanied personnel housing. These allowances shall be used during requirements determination in the initial outfitting for newly constructed UEPH/UOPH, and for the replacement/ augmentation of furniture in existing UPH's. Guidance for the procurement, management and control of PSE is provided in MCO P10150.1.

Transient Billeting. The transient mission is for the temporary billeting of temporary additional duty (TAD) personnel. It is supported primarily with appropriated money and supplemented with nonappropriated funds (NAF) from the billeting fund. This mission has no relationship with MWR hostess houses or any other MWR managed lodging. NAF's must be reinvested in transient billeting activities. Policy and guidance is provided in MCO P11000.22.

UNACCOMPANIED PERSONNEL HOUSING (UPH) QUESTIONS

1. Is there a designated UPH manager?

2. Are we organized to manage and assign UPH? Are changes needed?

3. For how many UPH quarters do we have assignment responsibility?

4. What is the capacity of UPH based upon the minimum standards of acceptability?

5. What is the maximum capacity of UPH at minimum health criteria
(i.e., 72 net square feet per recruit/90 net square feet for permanent personnel)?

6. What UPH support is available in the private community?

7. Do unaccompanied personnel receive services from the housing referral office in locating off-based housing?

8. Are the minimum allowances for personnel support equipment provided for UPH (officer and enlisted)?

9. Are routine and emergency maintenance requests answered in a timely manner?

10. Is a self-help maintenance program in effect that includes unaccompanied personnel?

11. Can any improvements be made to the self-help program?

12. Are unaccompanied personnel using the self-help facility?

13. Is vandalism a problem in UPH?

14. What are we doing to encourage occupants of UPH to conserve energy/resources?

15. What are we doing to encourage UPH occupants to properly care for the quarters?

16. How many complaints are received per month about UPH? What is the nature of the complaints? What corrective action is taken on complaints received?

17. Has the UPH Inventory and Utilization Data Report been filled out accurately and forwarded to the CMC (LFF-3) on a quarterly basis?

18. Have you provided a quality of life in the barracks to minimize the disparity between the bachelor and married Marine?

19. Are we using the Whole Room Concept/DoD Packaged Room Program to order PSE?

BILLETING FUND AND TRANSIENT BILLETING QUESTIONS

1. How many sets of quarters are used for transient billeting?
(CMC goal for adequate transient quarters is 75 percent)

2. Do we have VIP/distinguished guest quarters?

3. How much do we charge for transient quarters? (Rate per guidelines in MCO P11000.22, so that billeting fund does not operate at a loss.)

4. Do we accept the American Express credit card? (CG's decision).

5. Who manages the nonappropriated billeting fund? (Cannot be the Comptroller MCO P11000.22, paragraph 2507.3.)

6. How many employees, working in transient billeting, are paid with nonappropriated billeting funds?

7. Are transient billeting fund budgets briefed and approved by the activity commander? Have copies of 2d Qtr and year end budgets been forwarded to the CMC (LFF-3) for information?

FAMILY HOUSING

General Management. It is the Marine Corps desire to provide the necessary support for the most important "Quality of Life" issue, the living conditions of our Marines and their families. It is DoD policy that "Excellent facilities and services shall be provided for all military members, their families, and eligible civilians...Family housing facilities shall be operated and maintained to a standard that protects the facilities from deterioration and provides conformable places for our people to live." and "...Military family housing amenities and services should reflect contemporary United States living standards for similar categories of housing."

The Marine Corps has six specific goals for family housing: (1) maintain, repair and modernize our current housing inventory; (2) maintain, repair and modernize our housing infrastructure; (3) eliminate environmental hazards; (4) eliminate our deficit; (5) build housing support facilities to enhance quality of life (i.e., community centers, welcome centers, housing offices, self-help, warehouses, recreational facilities, etc.); and (6) improve housing referral services.

Requirements Survey. Family Housing requirements are reviewed annually by a market analysis directed by HQMC for those activities in the 5-year construction program. However, you may request a family housing market analysis anytime you feel an analysis would help justify a need. The housing problem is considered as an area, not merely an on-base, problem. Much of the basic data for the family housing market analysis is also used in the annual bachelor housing requirements estimate; therefore, both documents should be coordinated at your activity.

Private Housing. DoD, DON, and CMC directives require that primary reliance be placed on the use of private housing in the community to meet the needs of military families. Your housing referral service (HRS) or a joint/coordinated housing referral service, where necessary, is established to help military families locate private rental housing. This system is effective only if military personnel report to the housing referral office on arrival in the area, as required.

Housing Assignment. The instruction covering the designation of quarters, eligibility for housing assignment, and utilization of military housing is covered by MCO P11000.22. CMC (LFF) approves the designation of commanding officer quarters and general officer quarters (GOQ).

GOQ. Congressional limitations for each GOQ is $25,000 for maintenance and repair per year; operation costs are not capped. GOQ's with maintenance and repair projects exceeding this limitation must be approved in the President's budget. Those that are approved by Congress, must be executed in the year of approval. The congressional language prohibits out-of-cycle requests except in case of emergency or safety-related situations. The DC/s I&L has been delegated the authority to establish and adjust spending limitations when the limitations are within the congressional mandated threshold of $25,000 for maintenance and repair. The DC/s I&L has established the maintenance and repair limitations at $20,000 per year for those GOQ's which do not anticipate exceeding the congressional limitation. Each GOQ occupant should be aware of the Congressional limitation, and all the costs associated with operation and maintenance of their quarters.

Funding Support. Family housing funds are authorized and appropriated by Congress through the Family Housing Navy and Marine Corps (FHN&MC) appropriation. Both the Congress and DoD have imposed a number of controls governing the utilization of family housing funds. For example, FHN&MC O&M funds cannot be used for any purpose other than the operation, maintenance, repair, incidental improvement, and leasing of family housing. Conversely, plant property, and activity O&MMC funds cannot be used to operate or maintain family housing. Family housing funds must be used to maintain common areas when such common areas are included on the family housing plant account. Other restrictions are specified in pertinent DoD, NAVCOMPT, and CMC directives.

Approval Limitations. Current approval levels:

Category	Cost Limitations	Approval Authority	Submitted By
1. O&M incidental improvement (R-1 Projects)			
Any one unit within a fiscal year	$0-2000/unit; $0-150,000/ project	Act Cmdr	Act Cmdr
	$2,001- $150,000- 300,000/proj	HQMC	Act Cmdr
2. Annual improve- ment (R-2 Projects)	(See note 1.) $0-$50,000/unit; $500K/project	HQMC	HQMC

3.	Repairs			
	Cost per unit in any 12-month period	Up to $12,000/ unit; $0-300,000/ project	Act Cmdr	Act Cmdr
		$12,001-15,000/ unit; $300,001-3M/ project	HQMC	Act Cmdr
		Over $15,000/ unit	Congress	CMC
		Over$3M/Project	ASN (I&E)	CMC
4.	Furnishings			
	Special allowance items for special command positions	$3,500 initial issue $400 maintenance, repair, replacement in 1 year	CMC	CMC
5.	Demolition	None; all must be submitted for approval	OSD	CMC

NOTES: 1. Programmed on annual basis using CMC priority. Selected projects approved by OSD for legislative consideration and authorization as a program. Separate line-item congressional approval required for all improvements projects exceeding $50,000/unit or $1M/project. SecNav approval required on projects of $500K or more. No local authority.

FAMILY HOUSING QUESTIONS

1. Who is the HQMC point of contact for housing? Do they work with us regularly?

2. How are we organized to manage and assign quarters? Is this satisfactory? Any changes needed?

3. For how many quarters do we have assignment responsibility?

4. What are our waiting lists by rank and grade?

5. What is the community support housing situation?

6. Are there sufficient housing assets in the private community for the activity to house all of our married personnel? If not, what is being done to alleviate this condition?

7. Do our people get any assistance in locating off-base housing?

8. How effective is this Housing Referral Service (HRS) operation?

9. Has all on-base housing been inspected in the past year for maintenance and repair deficiencies?

10. How do BAQ and variable housing allowance (VHA) compare with local rental rates?

11. Do we have a long range maintenance plan for housing?

12. What are the limitations on use of FHN&MC O&M funds for maintenance, repair, and improvements?

13. What adjustments can I make?

14. How large is our BMAR on housing?

15. Do we have adequate personnel for quarters support?

16. Do we have a complete inspection and long range plan for improvements?

17. What are our funding problems, if any?

18. What active or proposed requirements/projects for improvements or repairs to quarters do we have?

19. What approval authority has been delegated to me?

20. What are the approval levels at HQMC and above?

21. What are we doing to stimulate occupant interest and responsibilities for minor repairs and grounds upkeep?

22. What are we doing to encourage housing occupants to conserve energy/natural resources?

23. How many congressionals do we receive during the year on family housing? What is the nature of complaints?

24. How can we better inform or satisfy occupants to reduce complaints?

25. Are GOQ's expenses within the CMC approved ceiling?

26. Is the occupant aware of the congressional limitations imposed upon GOQ's?

27. Do GOQ quarterly reports reflect all incurred costs for the period?

28. Are GOQ quarterly cost reports reviewed and signed by the occupant?

29. Is the occupant of a GOQ involved in the long range maintenance planning of the quarters?

30. Is the occupant of a GOQ informed prior to a request for funds for his quarters?

NATURAL RESOURCES

As a commander of a Marine Corps activity you are responsible for developing and implementing a comprehensive program for the management of all the natural resources controlled by the activity. The program is to be developed in harmony with the military land use requirements of the activity, and neither should be mutually exclusive of the other. The program is normally managed by a natural resources and environmental affairs officer assigned to your staff.

The Natural Resources Management Program includes the following as appropriate:

      Land Use Planning

      Forest Management

      Fish and Wildlife Enhancement

      Soil and Water Conservation

      Agricultural Outleasing

      Outdoor Recreational Use of Natural Resources

      Protection of Endangered and Threatened Species

Program requirements are contained in MCO P5090.2, Environmental Compliance and Protection Manual. The basic document for the program is the Integrated Natural Resources Management Plan which is developed locally with the assistance of cooperating Federal and State conservation agencies.

NATURAL RESOURCES QUESTIONS

1. Has a natural resources and environmental affairs office been established?

2. Do we thoroughly consider natural resources in assessing the impact of actions on the environment, and is the natural resources staff consulted in performing the assessment?

3. Have we assigned responsibility for coordinating provisions of the Endangered Species Act with Federal, State, and local authorities?

4. Is our Integrated Natural Resources Management Plan complete and current? Has the activity executed a cooperative plan with appropriate federal and state agencies?

5. Is the plan systematically integrated with military and overall activity plans?

6. Are all tenant commands and local conservation interests aware of the program and actively contributing to its implementation? Are there any conflicting interests?

7. Are we identifying and supporting program requirements and actually accomplishing planned work?

8. Have we established regulations to control the harvest of fish and game per Federal and State hunting, fishing, and trapping regulations?

9. Do we participate in the Secretary of Defense Natural Resources Conservation Awards Program?

ENVIRONMENTAL QUALITY

ENVIRONMENTAL MANAGEMENT. Your activity is subject to all applicable Federal, State, and local substantive (e.g., effluent limitations) and procedural (e.g., permits) environmental regulations. These regulations form the basis for the operation of facilities to control pollution from sources such as:

Water pollution control: sewage and industrial waste water treatment plants, wash racks, stormwater runoff, and boiler blow-down.

Air pollution control: heating plants, incinerators, vehicles, fuel handling facilities, degreasing equipment, and painting facilities.

Solid waste control: landfills, hazardous waste generation and storage sites, and resource recovery operations.

Pest control: mixing and storage facilities, pesticide use and disposal.

Failure to comply with these requirements can subject commanders to civil and/or criminal liabilities and can result in issuance of cease and desist orders, civil suits, and adverse publicity. Projects within your O&MMC minor construction authority threshold to correct environmental deficiencies can be funded locally. Those projects above the local authority thresholds will compete for limited centrally managed resources. Pollution abatement projects of MCON scope must now compete with all other MCON requirements. It is essential for the command to submit these projects with sufficient priority to assure funding. Priorities should balance mission requirements and regulatory pressures you may face. Facilities projects guidance on environmental management projects is found in MCO P11000.5, MCO P5090.2, and MCO P11000.12. Environmental project information is contained in COMPTRAK, a database used by the CMC (LFL) and installations to track project and compliance information. The U.S. Marine Corps Commander's Guide to Environmental Compliance and Protection is also a comprehensive reference on environmental management.

Environmental Planning. The National Environmental Policy Act (NEPA), through the President's Council on Environmental Quality (CEQ), requires the assessment of all proposed actions for environmental impact. MCO P5090.2 requires you to have an environmental quality/impact review board to assist the commander in determining the significance of this impact. If the proposed action is not categorically excluded, you must prepare an environmental assessment (EA). The conclusion (finding) of the EA may be the requirement for an Environmental Impact Statement (EIS) for release to the Environmental Protection Agency and the public, or formal public issuance of a Finding of No Significant Impact (FONSI).

Hazardous Waste Management. Environmental contamination caused by inadequately disposed of hazardous wastes (HW) has raised public concern and led to increased regulatory control. Substantial liabilities, both civil and criminal, are possible if HW are improperly managed. The cost for hazardous waste disposal is rapidly increasing as regulations become more stringent and choices for acceptable disposal methods decrease Proper disposal will become an increasingly important part of your operating budget. Activities should institute proactive efforts to minimize hazardous waste generation. A two-phased approach to HW management includes a program to track currently generated HW using a manifest system and a program to assess possible environmental contamination caused by previous waste disposal practices. This program, called the installation restoration program includes an evaluation of your activity's past disposal practices, identification of possible disposal sites, an assessment of contaminant migration, and the development of corrective projects where contamination is discovered. The DRMO and the NAVFAC EFD play key roles in these programs.

ENVIRONMENTAL QUALITY QUESTIONS

1. What is our compliance status?

2. Is adequate support being provided by the NAVFAC EFD?

3. Who are the members of the Environmental Impact Review Board and how often do they meet?

4. What enforcement actions have we received?

5. What enforcement actions are outstanding?

6. What is being done to resolve outstanding enforcement actions?

7. Do we currently have any Compliance Agreements or Consent Orders?

8. How is our working relationship with the regulatory agencies?

9. Have NEPA requirements been addressed and documented for proposed actions?

10. Have mitigation measures been carried out?

11. When was our last Environmental Compliance Evaluation (ECE) performed? By whom?

12. What deficiencies were found?

13. Do we have a plan of action and milestones developed for deficiencies?

14. What is being done to correct those deficiencies?

15. What is the status of our permits?

16. Is COMPTRAK being used?

QUESTIONS FOR YOUR PUBLIC WORKS OFFICER

1. What construction and repair projects are planned or in progress to address environmental deficiencies?

2. Are these projects being coordinated with the environmental coordinator and facilities maintenance officer?

3. Has the proper documentation for each project been provided to CMC (LFL/LFF) and the supporting EFD?

FOOD SERVICE AND SUBSISTENCE

The food service program objectives are based upon Department of Defense Directive (DODD) 1338.10, Department of Defense Food Service Program. These objectives are:

    a. Ensure the efficient and effective use of personnel, materials, and financial resources while providing the highest standards of food service.

    b. Provide standard methods, techniques, and procedures in food service operations and an auditable accounting system.

    c. Provide continuous training for food service personnel in all phases of food service operations. The individual training standards (ITS) system for food service Occupational Field 33 (officer and enlisted) and subsistence Military Occupational Specialty (MOS) 3381 (Food Service Specialist) are contained in MCO 1510.72 ITS's ensure that all Marines who have the same job are provided a common base of performance oriented training.

Facilities. As the installation commander you should ensure that Marines aboard your installation are provided with food which is of good quality, sufficient quantity, and well prepared. Messhalls provide Marine Corps enlisted personnel who are authorized Subsistence in Kind (SIK) with wholesome, nutritional meals using the Basic Daily Food Allowance (BDFA). Messhalls will be designed to assure the latest state-of-the-art equipment, a pleasant environment with decor consistent with that found in first-class commercial cafeterias and fast food restaurants.

Criteria and Standards. Basic allowance for subsistence (BAS) is an amount of money, prescribed and limited by law, which is paid to military members in lieu of subsistence at Government expense. BAS falls into three categories: BAS when SIK is not available; commuted rations when a Government messhall is available but permission to subsist separately has been granted; and BAS when assigned to duty under emergency conditions where no Government messhall is available. Enlisted Marines are entitled to rations for each day on active duty, except when they are authorized BAS or per diem instead of subsistence.

Surcharge/Neal Rate. The surcharge/meal rate is a monetary amount charged officers, civilians, and certain enlisted members who eat in appropriated fund messhalls. Such rates are established at a level sufficient to provide reimbursement of operating expenses and food costs to the appropriations concerned.

Fiscal. The O&MMC subsistence appropriation covers all SIK costs. SIK is an entitlement provided to all active duty enlisted personnel who do not receive BAS (Title 10 USC 6081 (a)).

Funds provided under this category are to be used specifically for procurement of food items in support of the general mess, flight meals, packaged operational rations, and fuel bar trioxane used to heat the meals ready-to-eat (MRE). Financial responsibility for the food service systems is vested in the installations commander by the Marine Corps Manual, paragraph 4301, and MCO P10110.14. This responsibility cannot be delegated to a subordinate commander.

Food Management Teams. Food management teams render assistance to the installation commanders in raising the quality of food service, achieving economy, and increasing effectiveness of the food service program.

Civilian Contract Feeding. Civilian contractor employees should accomplish all food service attendant tasks, except at locations where civilians are not available and during exercises or contingency operations. When a strike or other contractor work stoppage occurs without warning, you may determine that assigning military personnel as messmen, cashiers, and verifiers are required to support the activity mission.

Veterinary Medical Support. Under your direction, the U.S. Army Veterinary Service is responsible for conducting food inspections of subsistence supplies procured by Marine Corps appropriated and nonappropriated fund activities.

Marine Corps Food Management Information System (MCFMIS). The use of MCFMIS is mandatory at all Marine Corps messhalls, to include full contract facilities. MCFMIS training must be established at the food service level to ensure personnel are able to operate the system completely and properly.

FOOD SERVICE QUESTIONS

1. What value was received from the last visit by the Food Service Management Team?

2. What is the current status of the civilian mess contract?

3. How accurate have subsistence budget forecasts been?

4. Have we, the command, fallen within the established financial parameters on the Subsistence Operational Analysis Report (SOAR)?

5. Does the local master menu comply with Marine Corps nutrition standards?

6. Do we have a fast food/take-out service?

7. What is our SIK attendance rate?

8.   Who was the recent chef of the quarter?

9.   Do we possess a long-range equipment replacement plan?

10   Are patron surveys used to solicit customer recommendations?

11.   Do using units have representation on the menu planning board?

12.   What are the actual per-meal costs by messhall?   (Per-meal costs are arrived at by capturing all annual costs, (i.e., messhall attendant contracts, military and civilian cooks wages, equipment, utilities, repair and maintenance of facility) and dividing by the total annual meals served.)

13.   Do we have a long range plan for the maintenance/upgrade of our messhalls and messhall equipment?

GARRISON PROPERTY

The garrison property program manages all Government personal property used to support the operations of Marine Corps installation and tenant activities. Fleet Marine Force (FMF) deployable equipment assigned to or in the possession of operating forces and moved with the unit when it rotates or deploys is not classified or reported as garrison property.

For accounting purposes, garrison property is categorized as either plant or minor property. Items with a unit cost greater than $50,000 are plant property. Items with a unit cost less than $50,000 are minor property.

Personnel Support Equipment (PSE). PSE provides for cyclic replacement of furniture, furnishings and equipment for existing bachelor quarters (BQ), messhalls (furniture and furnishings only), and offices. Facilities must be furnished to achieve the minimum standards of adequacy using the allowances established for BEQ/BOQ/offices. The Department of the Navy's replacement goal is 7 years. The PSE Annual Inventory Report is due to the CMC (LFS) by 15 September of each year. This report is used to formulate the annual PSE O&MMC allocation plan for each activity as well as justifications throughout the entire budget cycle to include the POM.

Food Preparation and Serving Equipment (FPSE). The FPSE program provides major equipment support for messhalls at CONUS and overseas installations. FPSE refers to all major equipment used in messhall galleys, serving and dining areas, and food service schools. Procure expendable items not defined as FPSE (utensils, linens, dishes, and paper products) with local O&M funds. FPSE funds are allocated based on the requirements each activity submits for each budget year.

Messhall Facility Improvement Program (MFIP). The MFIP is designed to improve the utility and appearance of messhalls throughout the Marine Corps. The program evaluates messhalls on a 5- to 6-year rotation basis to determine MFIP requirements. MFIP projects include funding for minor construction or repair, expense and investment equipment, a decor package, and installation costs. Submit projects annually to the CMC (LFS/LFF).

Collateral Equipment in Military Construction (CE MCON). CE MCON is the initial outfitting of furniture, furnishings, and equipment for a project generated through new construction or expansion of a facility. Projects performed in conjunction with MILCON, UMC, or JFIP result in a change in facility function, operation, or an improvement in physical condition. Your Facilities Branch or Division will submit, for each project, the CE MCON requirements on a separate NAVFAC-4-11010/32, along with the DD Form 1391, to the CMC (LFL) with a copy to the CMC (LFS) and the appropriation sponsor for other equipment, as required. After the initial submission, you will forward the updated CE MCON list to the CMC (LFS) with a copy to the appropriation sponsor for any other equipment.

Warehouse Equipment. Policy for procurement of warehouse equipment to support Warehouse Modernization projects is in MCO 4450.10 and NAVSUP PUB 529. Submit project requirements annually to the CMC (LFS).

GARRISON PROPERTY QUESTIONS

1. Are we participating in the MFIP?

2. Is our garrison property identified with barcoded labels?

3. Has PSE in BEQ/BOQ been upgraded on a cyclic basis (7- to 10-years)?
4. Does PSE in offices comply with the table of allowance for individuals?
5. Do we have a PSE refurbishment plan?

6. Does our FPSE budget include state-of-the-art and replacement equipment?

7. Have all messhalls been upgraded through the MFIP in the past 7 years?

8. Have all equipment requirements been included in the CE MCON lists (NAVFAC-4-11010/32)?

9. Have all CE MCON requirements been identified to the correct appropriation sponsor? (e.g., general purpose PSE and equipment - LFS; automated data processing equipment (ADPE) - CCTAR; security equipment - POS; etc.)

10. Have all our warehouses been modernized with state-of-the-art storage and packaging equipment?

11. Has replacement of obsolete plant account investment items been budgeted for in the Command Support Equipment (CSE) PMC budget?

GARRISON MOBILE EQUIPMENT

Garrison Mobile Equipment (GME). GME is used to perform in-garrison services, transportation and maintenance functions at Marine Corps Installations. It consists of passenger and cargo vehicles, materials handling and engineer equipment, and railway rolling stock. GME is commercially available equipment and is not intended for tactical use.

GME QUESTIONS

1. Has a single GME fleet manager been assigned for the operation and maintenance of GME?

2. Have GME utilization goals been established in terms of a productive index, such as miles driven and hours operated that will allow for effective use of equipment and validation of allowances?

3. Have permissible operating distances (POD) been established for GME and is POD included in the unit's GME SOP?

TRAFFIC MANAGEMENT

Traffic Management Office (TMO). The TMO is responsible for making arrangements and preparing necessary documentation to move Marine Corps personnel and material. They use the appropriate mode of transportation including rail, truck, air, ocean, intermodal (containers), and small package express companies. For outbound freight, the TMO arranges commercial transportation, prepares shipment documentation, and loads shipments on carrier's equipment. For inbound freight, the TMO receives and visually inspects for transportation damages, assembles, and distributes material consigned to you. The TMO receives and processes applications for movement of household goods, provides for temporary and nontemporary storage, and makes arrangements for delivery, pickup, and packing of household goods for all eligible personnel requesting assistance. The TMO provides passenger transportation services to military and civilian personnel. The TMO is responsible to ensure that the personnel and material are moved in the most efficient and economical manner. The TMO also provides transportation and traffic management technical advisory services, does traffic studies and analyses, and supports carrier negotiations in securing new or advantageous rates, routes, and services. The TMO executes entitlement authorized by order writing activities/other competent authority per the JFTR/JTR. TMO's can interpret entitlement but they do not provide entitlement.

The typical TMO provides the following functions:

Freight

Arrange transportation, document and coordinate loading outbound material, including hazardous material, via appropriate mode of transportation.

Obtain service from USTRANSCOM's Transportation Component Commands (TCC'S); i.e., Air Mobility Command (AMC), Military Sealift Command (MSC), Military Transportation Management Command (MTMC).

Receive, inspect, and distribute incoming freight, cargo, and equipment.

Administer DoD and local quality control programs.

Provide packaging, packing and preservation (PP&P) support (exception: sites where 1st, 2d, and 3d FSSG is controlling PP&P function).

Passenger

Arrange commercial and military passenger airlifts worldwide.

Arrange port call of overseas passengers.

Arrange unit moves/groups not coordinated by COMMARFORLANT/PAC/MARFORRES strategic mobility offices.

Arrange bus and air charters.

Administer commercial travel office contract.

Personal Property

Counsel eligible Marine Corps and other service-sponsored personnel regarding their entitlement.

Book household goods, baggage, private owner vehicles (POV), boats, and mobile home shipments.

Arrange for the shipment, reception, and storage of household goods.

Administer quality control programs.

Assist service members in filing their claims.

Budget

Certify vouchers.

Forecast annual shipping requirements.

Use allocated dollars efficiently.

Justify additional requirements when allocation is going to be exceeded.

Submit estimated obligations of O&MMC, TOT to CMC (LFT-1).

TRAFFIC MANAGEMENT QUESTIONS

1. Are all TP-2 priority cargo (not including exceptions) shipped via surface mode?

2. Are all shipping requests via AMC channel aircraft weighing 150 lbs or more challenged?

3. What shipping/receiving capabilities do we have on base? Heavy lift, truck, water, etc.?

4. Do we have central receiving and who does the reception function?

5. What quality control and training programs and record keeping

of that training do we have in place to ensure compliance with all Federal, State, local, and international laws and regulations; e.g., hazardous materials?

6. What actions have we taken or plan to take to improve the efficiency and effectiveness of our freight operation; e.g., automation of processes, standardization, etc.?

7. Any problem with servicing the units/activities on our base?

8. Do we have any vacancies in key positions?

9. What do AMC, MSC, and MTMC do for us? Any problems with their service?

10. Do we have any guaranteed traffic awards covering our base? If not, why not? If we do, how is the service?

11. Do we maximize the use of containers? Do we own any containers? Do the tenant FMF Commands have containers?

12. Do we provide travel service to other than Marines?

13. Do we use PRAMS for the ANC flights? How does it work?

14. How do we help with unit moves (i.e., UDP, contingencies and exercises)?

15. What capability do we have to meet passenger mobilization requirements (charter buses, etc.)?

16. Does the Commercial Travel Office (CTO) who provides official travel support also provide leisure travel service?

17. Do we get any discounts? If so, where does the money go?

18. Are we satisfied with the CTO? Must improvements be made?

19. Who is authorized to travel business class?

20. Can TAD travelers participate in frequent flyer programs? If so, can they use credits earned for upgrades to business class?

21. What is TOPS? How does it improve service to our Marines?

22. What is the backlog for outbound shipments?

23. What is TQAP? How will this affect current procedures? What is a Tonnage Distribution Record (TDR)?

24. How many claims do we assist in processing yearly?

25. How many Marines are using the do-it-yourself (DITY) move program?

26. Does the commercial industry provide adequate service to our Marines?

27. What is the weigh/reweigh program? Is it effective?

28. How do we arrive at the estimated charges for shipping? Are the figures realistic and annotated correctly on all government bill of lading (GBL)?

29. How often do we use the Navy opportune lift and TP-4 in a month, year? How much are we saving?

30. What are our Second Destination Transportation (SDT) controls and how are we tracking our SDT obligations to ensure these controls are not exceeded without CMC approval?

31. Are O&MMC, TOT obligations submitted to MCLB, Albany (Code 470) via automated means; i.e., TMS?

32. Are the TMO (MOS 3112) Marines being cross trained? Are they getting the formal training they need? Do all MOS 3112 SGT's and below have a 4,000 pound forklift license?

33. Is the TMO's interface with the Senior Tenant Command's Strategic Mobility Office (SMO)/Embarkation Office sufficient to ensure strong coordination between them during deployment?

34. Are tenant commands FSSG/CSSG MOS 3112 Marines trained in freight and passenger functions sufficient to ensure forward deployed TMO DET's can perform the functions in theater?

35. Does the TMO have people trained in JOPES and GTN?

INSTALLATION EXCELLENCE PROGRAMS

Several programs or initiatives aimed at promoting installation excellence and facilitating the sharing of resources and successes are coordinated from the Office of the Assistant Deputy Chief of Staff for Installations (Facilities) (LF). As well, issues and initiatives affecting the supporting establishment often cross departmental lines and are more often than not coordinated by LF in its advocacy role for the supporting establishment. The following are a few formalized programs of particular interest to the commander:

Annual DOD Installation Commanders' Conference. This conference is generally held in the Washington, DC area during the second quarter of the fiscal year. The conference is sponsored by the Office of the Secretary of Defense and co-hosted by each service on a rotational basis from year to year. It is attended by DoD installation commanders worldwide. It is usually structured so that OSD policy makers address the attendees in plenary sessions (1 day) on broad topical issues, preceded or followed by service break-out sessions (2 days). It is during these service-day sessions that the Marine Corps takes the opportunity of having all base/station commanders together to discuss supporting establishment issues with the HQMC staff and to share successes among commanders.

Annual Commander in Chief's Installation Excellence Award. An OSD sponsored award competition recognizing the "best of the best" installation in each service and the Defense Logistics Agency. Presidentially proclaimed by President Reagan in 1984 and subsequently sanctioned by each President since, the award recognizes the efforts of the people who operate and maintain our installations and who have done the best with their resources to support the mission. The Secretary of Defense hosts an awards ceremony at the Pentagon during May each year to publicly recognize the winners. Winners receive a trophy, flag, and Presidential letter, and the Marine Corps winner also receives $200,000 to be used at the command's discretion. Nominations are due HQMC (LF) by the end of December each year for the reporting period ending 30 September. (MCO 5200.26 refers.)

Interservice Support and Joint Interservice Regional Support Groups (JIRSG). DoD activities are encouraged to share resources by providing interservice support to requesting DoD activities. Each base/station has a designated interservice support coordinator (ISC) who coordinates the development of interservice support agreements (ISA) documenting the service(s) being provided or received. JIRSG's have also been established in geographical regions to facilitate communication among DoD activities and with other Federal activities. JIRSG's consist of collocated DoD installations that join together to share ideas and seek opportunities for improving efficiencies. ISC's are

often the installations's representative to the local JIRSG and
work closely to network into the JIRSG resources. Participation
in JIRSG's is voluntary but encouraged for the obvious benefit of
tapping into resources and extending communications beyond
installation boundaries. OSD sponsors an annual worldwide
Interservice Support Conference that brings OSD, Service, and
installation ISC's together to discuss current issues and for
support agreement training. The CMC (LF) is the ISA/JIRSG focal
point for the Marine Corps. (DODI 4000.19 refers.)

POINTS OF CONTACT

FOR INSTALLATION MANAGEMENT AND POLICY

Responsible Code	Function	Telephone Number
LF	FACILITIES AND SERVICES DIVISION	0837
	POLICY AND DIRECTION	0830/0837
	EXCELLENT INSTALLATIONS POLICY	
LFF	FACILITIES BRANCH	0859/0864
	SPECIAL PROGRAMS	0859/0852
	FIRE PROTECTION	
	ENERGY/UTILITIES	
	RECYCLING	
	RPMA BUDGET/PROJECTS	0852/0859
	HOUSING	0864/0860
	POLICY/PROJECTS/BUDGETS	
	BACHELOR/FAMILY/GOQ	
	RPMA POLICY	0860/0864
	MAINTENANCE/SUPPLY SUPPORT	
	PRODUCTIVITY ENHANCEMENT	
	SERVICE CONTRACTS	
LFL	LAND USE AND MILITARY CONSTRUCTION BRANCH	0865/1002
	MILCON PLAN/PROGRAM	1002
	REAL ESTATE/ENCROACHMENT/ INVENTORY	0865
	BASE CLOSURE	0865
	NATURAL RESOURCES	0865
	ENVIRONMENT	2138
	MCRN PLAN/PROGRAM	1002
	FACILITIES PLANNING	1002
	NAF MILCON REQUIREMENT	1002
LFS	SERVICES BRANCH	0850/0835
	SPECIAL PROGRAMS	0835/0836
	GARRISON MOBILE EQUIPMENT	0847/0848
	GARRISON PROPERTY	0832/0835
	FOOD SERVICE AND SUBSISTENCE	0839/0840
LFT	TRAFFIC MANAGEMENT BRANCH	0861
	FREIGHT SECTION	0844/0845
	PASSENGER SECTION	0855/0856
	PERSONAL PROPERTY SECTION	0842/3
	BUDGET SECTION	0857

HQMC PREFIXES: COMMERCIAL (703) 696-XXXX DSN: 426-XXXX
HQMC FAX: LFF xxx-0849 LF/LFL xxx-1020 LFS xxx-0851
           LFT xxx-0841

INSTALLATION MANAGEMENT ABBREVIATIONS

ADPE	Automated Data Processing Equipment
AMC	Air Mobility Command
AWPL	Annual Work Plan
AWPR	Annual Work Program
AICUZ	Air Installation Compatible Use Zone
BAQ	Basic Allowance For Quarters
BAS	Basic Allowance For Subsistence
BDFA	Basic Daily Food Allowance
BFR	Basic Facility Requirement
BMAR	Backlog of Maintenance and Repair
BPA	Blanket Purchase Agreement
CEQ	President's Council on Environmental Quality
CG	Commanding General
CO	Commanding Officer
CINCLANTFLT	Commander in Chief Atlantic Fleet
CINCPACFLT	Commander in Chief Pacific Fleet
CMC	Commandant of the Marine Corps
CTO	Commercial Travel Office
CULT	Common User Land Transportation
DC/S I&L	Deputy Chief of Staff for Installations and Logistics
DASD (I)	Deputy Assistant Secretary of Defense, Installations
DEIS-II	Defense Energy Information System Report Number 2
DGQ	Distinguished Guest Quarters
DITY	Do-it-Yourself
DoD	Department of Defense

DON	Department of the Navy
DRIS	Defense Regional Interservice Support
DRMO	Defense Reutilization and Marketing Office
DUERS	Defense Utility and Energy Reporting System
EA	Environmental Assessment
EAR	Energy Audit Report
ECIP	Energy Conservation Investment Program
EFD	Engineering Field Division
EUIP	Energy and Utilities Initiatives Program
EIS	Environmental Impact Statement
EPS	Engineering Performance Standards
ES	Emergency and Service Work
FACSO	Facilities Systems Office
FEMP	Federal Energy Management Program
FHMA,N&MC	Family Housing Management Account, Navy-Marine Corps
FONSI	Finding of No Significant Impact
FM	Facilities Maintenance
FMO	Facilities Maintenance Officer
FPE	Fire Protection Engineer
FPSE	Food Preparation and Serving Equipment
FSR	Facilities Support Requirements Planning Document
GBL	Government Bill of Lading
GME	Garrison Mobile Equipment
GOQ	General Officer Quarters
GSA	General Services Administration
GT	Guaranteed Traffic

GTN	Global Transportation Network
HRS	Housing Referral Service
HQMC	Headquarters, Marine Corps
HW	Hazardous Waste
ID/QTC	Indefinite Delivery/Quantity Type Contract
IRBAR	Inventory, Requirements, Budget, and Replacement
ISA	Interservice Support Agreement
ITS	Individual Training Standards
JOPES	Joint Operational Planning and Execution System
LF	Facilities and Services Division
LFF	Facilities Branch
LFL	Land Use and Military Construction Branch
LFS	Services Branch
LFT	Traffic Management Branch
LRMP	Long Range Maintenance Plan
MCON	Military Construction, Navy
MCON CE	Military Construction, Navy Collateral Equipment
MCNR	Military Construction Naval Reserve
MFIP	Messhall Facility Improvement Plan
MILCON	Military Construction
MLUMP	Multiple Land Use Management Plan
MOS	Military Occupational Specialty
M&R	Maintenance and Repair
MRE	Meals Ready-To-Eat
MRP	Maintenance of Real Property
MSC	Military Sealift Command

MTMC	Military Traffic Management Command
MWR	Morale, Welfare, and Recreation
NAF	Nonappropriated Fund
NAFI	Nonappropriated Fund Instrumentality
NAVFAC	Naval Facilities Engineering Command
NAVSUP	Naval Supply Systems Command
NEPA	National Environmental Policy Act
NFADB	Navy Facilities Assets Data Base
NFESC	Naval Facilities Engineering Services Center
O&MMC	Operations and Maintenance, Marine Corps Appropriation
OSD	Office of Secretary of Defense
P&CO	Purchasing and Contracting Officer
PCS	Permanent Change of Station
POM	Program Objectives Memorandum
PPV	Public/Private Ventures
PRAMS	Passenger Reservation Automation Management System
PSE	Personnel Support Equipment
ROE	Report of Excess
ROICC	Resident Officer in Charge of Construction
RPI	Real Property Inventory
RPMA	Real Property Maintenance Activities
RPM/FHS	Real Property Maintenance/Family Housing System
SABRS	Standard Accounting, Budgeting, Reporting System
SDT	Second Destination Transportation
SecNav	Secretary of the Navy
SIK	Subsistence in Kind

SMO	Strategic Mobility Office
SIOH	Supervision, Inspection and Overhead
SWAR	Solid Waste Annual Report
TAD	Temporary Additional Duty
TMO	Traffic Management Office
TMS	Traffic Management System
TOPS	Transportation Operational Personal Property Standard System
TOT	Transportation of Things
TOP	Transportation of People
TP-2	Transportation Priority 2
TQAP	Total Quality Assurance Program
UCAB	Utilities Conservation and Appraisal Board
UCAE	Utilities Cost Accounting Report
UEPH	Unaccompanied Enlisted Personnel Housing
UOPH	Unaccompanied Officer Personnel Housing
USTRANSCOM	US Transportation Command
VHA	Variable Housing Allowance

www.ingramcontent.com/pod-product-compliance
Lightning Source LLC
Chambersburg PA
CBHW081141290526
45795CB00006B/2327